romany free

romany free

by Robert Vavra

paintings by Fleur Cowles

REYNAL & COMPANY
in association with
William Morrow & Company, Inc.
New York

Library of Congress Catalog Card Number 77-77315

ISBN 0-688-61193-1

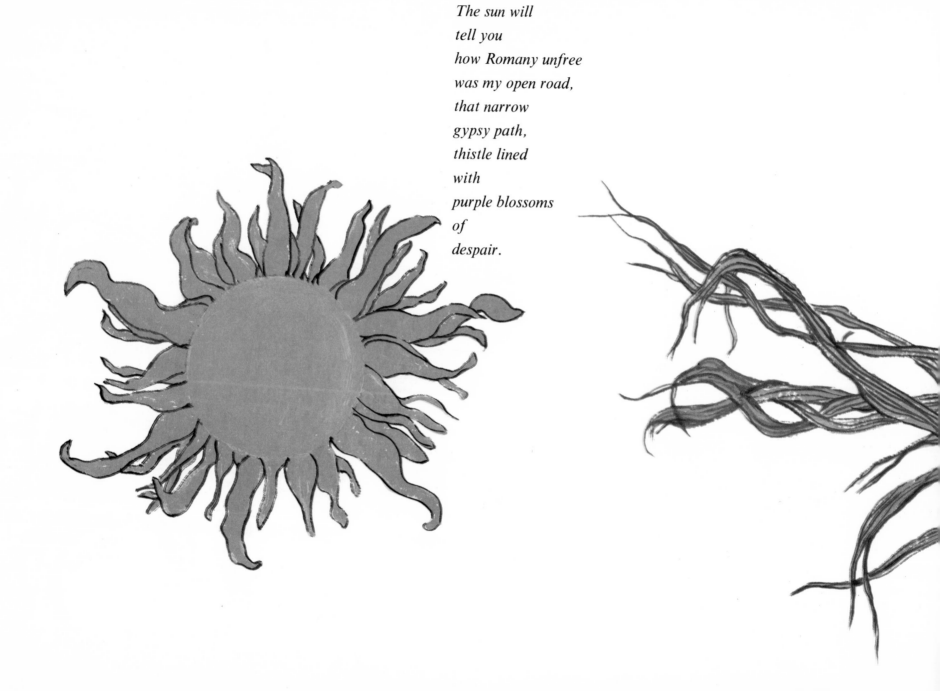

The sun will
tell you
how Romany unfree
was my open road,
that narrow
gypsy path,
thistle lined
with
purple blossoms
of
despair.

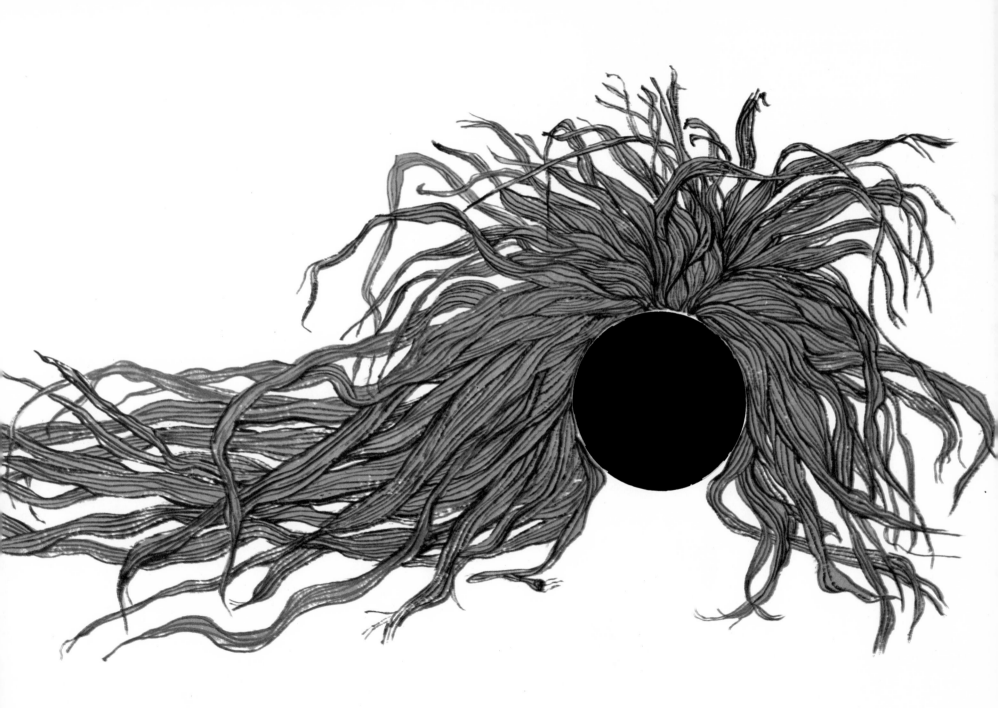

Sun,
I saw you
that
closing day,
listening while
eastern breezes
chorused in my
ears
evening songs
of
longed-for
solitude.

Sun,
you slowly rose
while those
sweet voiced
strangers
wove
through
my tangled
locks
nests of
curiosity.

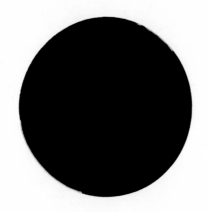

'Fly free!
Glide free!'
Their melodies
moved in me
secret wishes
for happiness.
'But how?'
I asked.
'My roots are
twined to
dancing bears
and copper.
I'm of the open road –
not the
sky.

'Stork,
high
and calm
on your tower,
tell me
what it is to
fly,
a delight
my featherless
arms
will never know.'

'To free
yourself
no wings
are needed,'
answered
the
lofty bird.
'Your mind
alone
will carry you
high.
Watch me
as I
rise –
tower, rocks and all -
floating
upward
through
azure skies.'

'Rest your head
on the grass,'
sang the birds
from my hair.
'Shut your eyes,
shut your eyes.
Feel the tide
at your feet.
Feel the surf
at your hands.
Feel the foam
around your brow –
and your breath
rolling smoother
than the waves
upon the
sand.

And with each
breath to the
breeze,
hear "free",
whisper "free",
until like
the stork
and
his tower
you're
drifting
unpossessed.'

Fragrant pollens
filtered through
my head.

Harmony blossomed
in
echoes
of
unknown beauty
    unknown beauty

       unknown beauty

Parrots
squawked
and shrieked
to
break
the calm.

But like
a
patient
seabird
contemplating
the morning sky
I remained
serene.

Crows and ravens
of
dark
distraction
tried
to screech
me back to
earth's
captivity.

'Cro-o-o!
Cro-o-o-o!'
a rooster
threatened
my new-found
peace,
as did the
clucking
nonsense
of a gaudy hen.

But the
only
call
to echo in
my ears
rose from
a lone
jungle fowl
as,
'Free!
Free!'
he released
the
forest night.

*Time
passed,
marked
by the
setting
sun.*

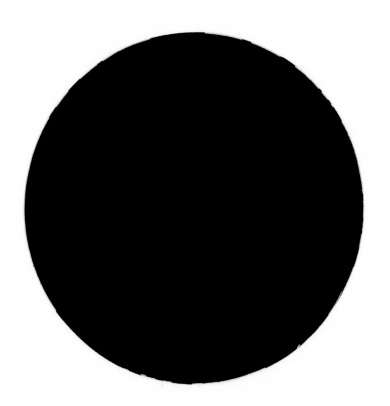

What face of new
delight
was mine.
What thoughts
sprouted
and blossomed
from that happy
basket-brow.
At peace with
all
about me
while sunshine
flowers
of new existence
cast out
their
fragrant
breath.

My head
was as light
and quick to sail
as the waiting
hawk.
Yet,
heavy was my
being
and centuries old,
like the
lone tusker
slaking his thirst
at
a
long
forgotten
pond.

*Hawk so
sharp-eyed,
resting now
from
flights
through
snowy cumulus.*

FLEUR·73

A day has
passed.
A month is
gone.
A year has
glided
by.
Sunset.
Sunrise.
They come
and
go
as gently
as
the
coooooooooing
of
enamoured doves.

Awareness
gliding currents
of
treasured
solitude
returns
singing
from
infinity.
The tide's
at my feet.
The surf's

on the sand.
The breeze is
moving gentler
than the
happiness
      in
        my
          hand.

OWNERSHIP OF PAINTINGS

AUTHOR'S NOTE

When TIGER FLOWER *had been written in 1967, but not yet published, Fleur Cowles and her husband, Tom Montague Meyer, travelled to Southern Spain where they joined me for several days in the Coto Doñana, that paradise of marshes and sand dunes that is probably Europe's most important wildlife refuge. And it was there in Doñana that Fleur first met Federico, a Mowgli-like gypsy boy who was the protagonist of my book* MILANE.

It was partly the wild child in Federico and partly the sensitive artist (he later became a painter like his adopted father John Fulton) that I think attracted Fleur and inspired her over the last ten years to do three or four paintings of him, several of which appear in this book. Seeing Federico playing in the marshes, free of the anxiety and violence of gypsy life, produced in all of us a state of calm. Admittedly, Doñana is a marvellous setting, one that I find as enticing today as I did on my first visit there fifteen years ago. It is an ideal place to search out one's self: contemplating sunsets, meditating at mid-day while egrets circle lazily overhead, or while stretched out under some giant cork oak, gazing upwards at an imperial eagle's nest. Such places of beauty, like the infinite offerings of nature found almost everywhere, evoke peace whether it be in a wild gypsy boy or a sophisticated Londoner – all of us have so-called 'open roads' from which we would best be free.

This little book, however, does not have a concrete theme or message. Fleur had her own ideas when she did the paintings, Federico must have been lost in completely different thoughts when his portraits were done. And my head took off on its own glide once the transparencies were spread before me.

So it should be with the reader, the viewer or the listener – free and happy sailing.

ROBERT VAVRA